Dear Purposeful Woman™

Courageous Words for You & Me

Vol. 1

Written by Shandice Stallworth

Seeds By Shandice
Publishing

Dear Purposeful Woman™
Vol. 1: Courageous Words for You & Me

Dear Purposeful Woman is a trademark of Dear Purposeful Woman, LLC

Published by Seeds By Shandice
www.seedsbyshandice.co/publishing

Edited by Leeza Ochsner and Katelyn Williams
Designed and illustrated by Lisa Pease

ISBN: 978-0-578-22985-0

This book is dedicated to every purposeful woman who sometimes, like me, needs a little nudge to walk in courage. *I see you.*

And to all the purposeful women who have nudged me along my journey . . . *I thank you.*

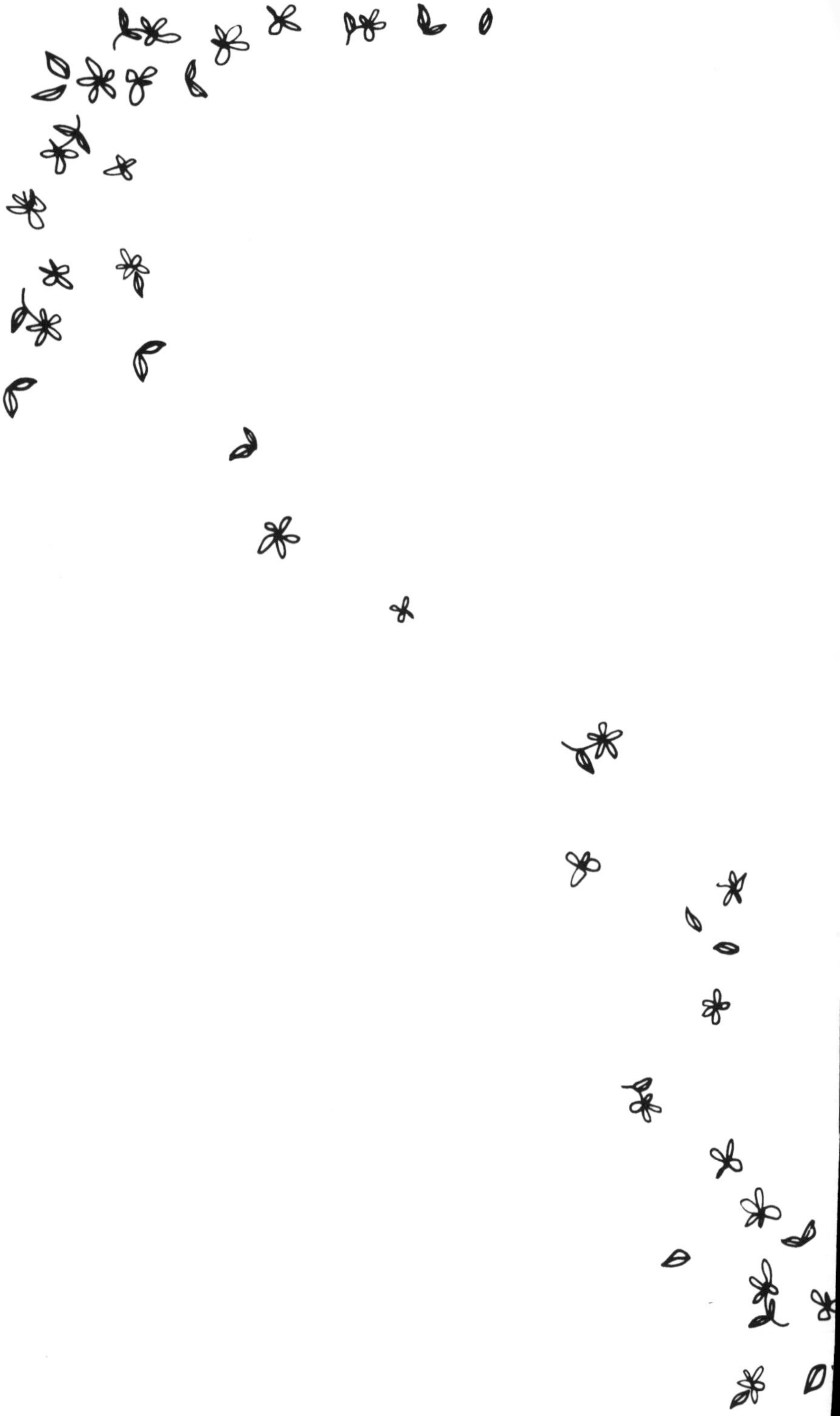

Dear Purposeful Woman,

I left so many words *unsaid* in my 20s.

Unaccepted. Unnurtured. Unheard.

So I decided to fill these empty pages with intimate words I once abandoned. Words written in endless journals, scribbled on random scraps of paper, and typed in more Google documents than I can humanly begin to count. I hope each word reminds us to courageously set our voices free because our stories matter, but first—they must matter to *us*.

I encourage you to use the empty pages and space around my words to write your own or draw images that inspire you to live freely and ignite your light within. If you wish to share my words or yours, tear out pages and gift them to fellow purposeful women as a loving reminder to move through the world with truth and courage. Some words may be for you, others may be for her; so gift them freely, as I bear witness, firsthand, to the power words hold to break chains within us all.

When I first wrote many of these words, I had no idea they would be read by you. Now I see that in all those moments I felt alone, unheard, and unseen, I was never truly alone. We were journeying together all along, across different time zones, sharing the same fears, facing our insecurities while uncovering our God-given purpose—*daily*.

And because of this deep knowing that we are so beautifully entwined, I lovingly present you with courageous words for you & me.

Much love, always,

Finally, she realized taking one courageous step forward meant so much more than endlessly planning to take ten steps all at once.

Joshua 1:9

Feel free to use the blank spaces throughout the book and
around my words to write and draw whatever comes to you.

1

Dear Purposeful Woman,

I know you struggle with being yourself at times.

You battle between expressing the true you and the "you" the world expects you to be. But you have a purpose, one that breaks through the walls of any image placed on your shoulders without your permission.

So today, *stand tall and be you.*

Be true to yourself—in life, in love, and in all of your pursuits, ***choose purpose.***

2 |

I was 26 years old when I first wrote the words on the page before this one. I created a pretty graphic in Canva, decorated with a thick black border and a perfectly drawn flower. I then added a touch of yellow to represent the light I hoped my words would spark. Instinctively I typed, *"Dear Purposeful Woman"* for the very first time. Three words I believed to capture the essence of purpose embodied in female form.

It was the fall of 2015, and I was a newlywed living in Statesboro, Georgia, with my husband, Rodger, after graduating with my master's degree. A born and raised Londoner with big dreams doing my very best to unwrap the present moment—despite my fears and insecurities, I was courageously ready to share my gifts with the world.

I know you struggle with being yourself at times. You battle between expressing the true you and the "you" the world expects you to be.

I continued typing as the words freely leaped from my fingertips. I hoped to encourage women who, like me, were passionate about living a purposeful life. Women who were ready to break free from their shackles and unapologetically embrace who God created them to be. And as much as I wrote those words for other women, I knew deep down I craved for those *same* words to touch and transform my soul too.

You have a purpose, one that breaks through the walls of any image placed on your shoulders without your permission.

I spent so much time questioning my purpose. Evaluating my speed, secretly craving acceptance, pressuring myself to perform, while simultaneously hanging my head down low. Too afraid of standing tall and firmly planting my feet in God's truth. I knew things had to change. I knew I couldn't thrive in the place to which I had mentally chained myself. It was time to break free. It was time to become the woman I *penned* to be.

So today, stand tall and be you.
Be true to yourself—in life, in love, and in all of your pursuits, *choose* purpose.

Drops pen, takes a break

I wish choosing purpose was easier done than said. Or maybe it is. Maybe we simply struggle with getting out of our own way so that we can authentically emerge into all we were already built to be.

Maybe it's the unnecessary act of running after purpose that makes things all the more complicated. The belief that we are incomplete until we scour the world to find the missing pieces of ourselves. But life has taught me the opposite. Purpose isn't something we endlessly search for; rather, it's something we uncover within ourselves, ignited through the process of truly becoming one with our God-given identity.

After searching in all the wrong places, I learned that I couldn't sincerely choose purpose without first choosing the Purpose-Giver. Choosing to be adopted as God's child. Choosing to believe the words He so graciously spoke over me while choosing to embrace His most simplistic and untampered idea of purpose—to glorify Him with my life. Nothing more. Nothing less. To simply and wholeheartedly be a walking, talking manifestation of His glory, so that others too may be drawn to His light and love.

Purpose is never too far away from us to grasp. Sometimes we simply need training to confidently hold its might without fearfully dropping it into a sea of our fears, doubts, and insecurities.

Recently, in the middle of one of my meltdowns, Rodger said to me, "Shandice, you need to release the pressure . . ." I thought I would have this thing all figured out by now; *ha*, clearly not. He went on to say, "You don't need to have all the answers. You can still help other women by sharing the lessons you've learned up until this point. This way they won't have to suffer through their process in the same ways you have."

One of the lies I have carried on my shoulders for way too long is that I am too broken to be used by God. I am not whole enough to help other women liberate the parts of themselves that our past, pain, and insecurities attempt to paralyze. I have carried the lie that I am incomplete, awaiting permission to be a vessel of hope and change. So each and every time I would put myself out there to share what my heart desired to release, my fears knew just the right words to seduce me back into my favorite hiding place.

But as I put the finishing touches on this book, something tells me I am not alone in this deceptive feeling. And though I still periodically wrestle with fear and doubt, an unwavering voice within is giving me the nudge I so desperately need to continue on this journey with courage. It is reminding me that women in transition write books too. Women who are afraid to fight but fight anyway, win battles too. You see, our weaknesses, though often despised, make room for God's unwavering strength.

Dear Purposeful Woman, you are purpose-filled even when you struggle to identify your purpose by name. You are courageous even when your fears work overtime to hold your courage captive. You are whole, even when you hurt. And you are never too broken to be used by God. So today, I stand tall with you, holding up your unapologetic cue to choose purpose—in life, in love, and in all of your pursuits.

3

There will be days where you don't feel strong enough to get out of bed in the morning.

As you attempt to remove the covers from your body, the weight of your inner battles will seduce you into covering your head, closing your eyes, and sweetly snuggling up to your sorrows. In those moments when life feels like too much to bear, your eyelids struggle to reopen, and your limbs feel paralyzed by the thought of what lies ahead . . . open your mouth instead.

Declare with all your heart and soul that, "This is the day that the Lord has made, and I will rejoice and be glad in it."

You are a child of the Most High God, and your bed will not steal any more of your days. So rise and shine, Dear Purposeful Woman; it's time to wake up and go live the life you were created to live.

4 |

I am created to **emerge**
stronger
and
wiser
in every season,
for God-given light cannot be hidden.

I
am
growing.

I
am
glowing.

I
am
building.

I am emerging.

5 |

We often desire the "glow up" without doing the work to *grow up.* But the glow is a byproduct of your growth. So don't get distracted by the glitter on your way towards the gold.

6

I so desperately wanted to bypass the refinement process necessary for cultivating a purposeful woman and sustaining a purposeful life—*from the inside out.*

For years, I anxiously ran ahead, believing I had something to prove to a world that was, in reality, too busy taking care of itself. Believing my worth was wrapped up in my work, knowing deep down I had to unravel that lie before it suffocated me.

Mum's words still ring in my ears: "Shandice, you don't need to chase anything in this world. Seek Him first and watch what so many spend their entire lives chasing to instead start seeking you." Echoed by the words of my therapist: "Shandice, you don't need to manipulate the world to get what you want; instead, focus on doing the inner work. It is the work that so many have mastered running away from."

I had reached the end of myself.

The only place left to run was right into the arms of God. To grow into my fullest potential, I had to forfeit this pressure-filled race I was running and instead start trusting Him with each step. I truly believe that when we surrender to His will, His work begins to penetrate our hearts, help us grow, and sustain us for the long game. When we stop attempting to have it all figured out to soothe our fear of failure, God's light ignites a truth so deep within that not even our darkest days can destroy it.

I think we all go through a stage of realization. Realizing that maybe speeding up will only tire us out for the journey ahead and that maybe we were never behind to begin with. Perhaps we made some bad decisions or settled somewhere along the way. But maybe we did the best we could with what we knew at the time. Maybe our perceived failures weren't failures after all, but rather the pathway to our present selves.

When all the realizations come flooding in, we mustn't drown in them. Instead, let's believe we are worthy of rescuing and learning from our mistakes. Don't leave yourself out in the cold, standing in the rain and punishing yourself for being imperfectly human. Take a real good look at your life and all that you have achieved and failed at, then realize you are not the sum of your failures or successes. You cannot let wild weeds dominate your garden when hopeful seeds remain in your hands, awaiting a chance to flourish.

I want us to stop beating ourselves up about every little thing. Instead, let's confidently move forward with the experiences and new knowledge we have gained along the way. Wisdom is a beautiful tool, an intentional gift often wrapped in regret. When we peel away each layer to reveal the truth, we often feel defeated, because we fell for the glitter of this world instead of wholeheartedly embracing the gold—the real substance of each day. We regret that we went looking in all the wrong places for treasures that were within us all along. Sometimes it hurts to realize just how human we are and how susceptible we are to sin. But God's grace <u>and</u> self-compassion have the power to heal that pain within us, once and for all.

I realized I wanted the prize without doing the hard inner work. I didn't want to go through the transformation process. I wanted more but continued to give only what I felt capable of producing on my own. How naïve of me to think a God-sized vision didn't require God. That walking in purpose, overcoming my pain, and pursuing wholesome things was a walk in the park. The more exposed I became to the reality of the process, the more I resisted it in search of another way.

Any way, but that way.

Have you ever found yourself saying, "Any way, but that way"?

You want to create [fill in the blank], but you don't want to be hurt by people. You don't want to lose friends, gain responsibility, start small, be laughed at, or make bold moves that scare you. You want to walk in purpose, *you really do*. But you don't know if you want to do the inner work. You don't want to die to the image you created of yourself years ago; it's comfortable and familiar even though it's not bearing fruit. You don't want to stand out, be seen as the oddball or the stuck-up one. You want to stay safe in your circle without disruption—*without being seen*.

I can share countless other "Any way, but that way . . ." scenarios, but I'm sure you have your very own. I'm sure there is something you're wrestling with that requires you to flex your courageous muscles. Once and for all, defeating the voice that keeps talking you out of surrendering to an unknown, terrifying process.

When it was time for me to start walking down the unfamiliar path of surrender, I was greeted by my strongest and scariest enemy. *Me*. With each step I took, I was attacked by words that pinned me against the wall and bullied me into believing I wasn't equipped to walk in freedom. The weight of those words was so heavy, so potent, so painful, that I often didn't know how to fight back. I was so afraid of unpinning myself from those vicious lies that, for a while, I chose to remain up against the wall. And it was in that moment of captivity that I realized I had spent so much time attempting to fight the naysayers and perceptions of this world that I became susceptible to the enemy within. The voice that sought to attack me was my own, a voice cultivated from my wounds, fears, doubts, and insecurities. I knew another voice lived within me, one cultivated by God's grace, courage, faith, and love, but I wasn't quite sure how to access it.

Even though time has passed, the realizations keep flooding my mind, and I honestly don't know what to do with them all at any one given moment. But what I do know is there isn't an easy way through this thing called life. Even with handouts and hand-ups, one of the greatest challenges we will experience is our ability to overcome ourselves. To defeat the unhealthy perception we so often hold dear to our hearts because it makes sense to who we once were. Growing past an outdated identity requires us to graciously accept new seeds of truth and create a safe space for those seeds to take root. If we desire to flourish beyond our past selves, we must first free ourselves from toxic self-judgment. We must choose love as we correct the errors of our ways, for condemnation does not breed freedom.

So I accepted that I struggled with control and only wanted to attempt things I knew I had the power to complete. But in my mind, I didn't feel as if I could complete anything, so I attempted nothing. *Catch-22*.

This realization needed a higher revelation, one that was God-birthed and ready to be watered by truth. Truth told me, "You must take 100% responsibility for your own life and take responsibility for being obedient to God's calls. You are responsible for how you respond to the trials you face. You are responsible for who you allow God to be in your life, but you are not responsible for being God." Alpha and Omega, Father and Friend—He is it all, so let *Him* be it.

As you swim through your own realizations, remember to courageously keep yourself afloat with the humbling truth that realizations are intended to be gifts from above. They are an opportunity, once investigated, to liberate you and prepare you to soar. Be open to the fact that some days you will realize your faults and other days you will realize your wings. So, as we continue through the pages of this book, let's make a vow to no longer drown in our past mistakes. It's time to stand up, kindly dust your shoulders off and boldly walk on water.

7 |

Breakthroughs begin beneath the surface. Be willing to get on your hands and knees to dig for the unseen, for you cannot uproot what you are unaware of.

8

I believe I am worthy of unbounded self-compassion. So I am patiently learning how to love myself without running away from the process.

9 |

It's possible to hold yourself accountable and treat yourself with human kindness. It's a simultaneous effort, rooted in love and grace.

10

Help me, Lord, to see the beauty in each step, to praise You in the midst of each transition, and to trust You beyond what I can see.

11

I struggled to embrace the steps.

My self-inflicted time crunch did nothing more than temporarily feed my fears and insecurities.

I was exhausted. Trying to keep up with toxic self-expectations becomes tiring after a while, doesn't it? Ignoring the needs of your spirit only to chase fleeting validation birthed out of your wounds.

I felt like I had something to prove. I needed to make it known that I wasn't just this shy girl from London who struggled to speak with confidence. I was going to change the world with my words. I was going to write book after book after book to help liberate women, who, like me, sometimes needed a nudge to walk in courage. And as sweet-willed as my intentions were, they were birthed out of a sour spot, a painful place that had yet to be acknowledged with care and unbounded love.

The pain would secretly whisper to my heart, *"Shandice, you don't have what it takes to reach the heights you dream of reaching."* And instead of addressing the quiet noise, I ran further and further away from it and into any and everything that would welcome me—on a quest to prove it wrong.

I ran into things I felt no real connection to, and timelines that didn't take into account the sacred work that God was doing within me. I think it's fair to say we should allow running to remain a form of exercise and not a means for journeying through life. How else will you get to smell the roses, breathe in the everyday moments, and surrender to the process of becoming? So that when those moments slip away, you are left with soulful memories birthed out of your ability to simply *be.*

12

Abundant joy is yours to embody even when sorrow seeps through your pores.

Love is yours.

Laughter is yours.

Internal and external success is yours.

Abundance doesn't discriminate, so be intentional about the words you speak and the thoughts you think. Resist the urge to hold yourself back to bring forth the lie that "lack" is all you can afford.

13 |

Start each day with courageous vibes, a grateful heart, and an authentic willingness to make a difference in the areas God has called you to.

14

If you let it, fear will make a home in your inner thoughts, paint the walls of your mind, and furnish it with lies. It will become a comfortable resting place that cannot awaken the woman you truly are. While we cannot control when fear shows up at our door, we can refuse it entry. We can turn it away and make sure it knows its place, so it no longer has the power to hijack our inner narrative.

Declare: Fear will not be my headline; fear will not be the legacy I leave behind.

Today,
release the clutter
strip the walls
paint them with truth
then open the doors
let in the light
let in the love
and renew your mind with words from above.

15

Courage is an act of love, and love is an act of courage.

They require one another to live in us and flow through us—*freely.*

16 |

When you look God's love in the eye, you'll see it holds no bounds. It is big enough to cover your weaknesses and strong enough to knock down your fears.

His love is forever present. His love is for all to feel and see.

God's love is here.

17

Fear,

you will no longer hold my story captive.

God's love is here.

18

Fear is paralyzing.

Do you remember the first moment you were aware of yourself? Your hair, your skin, your walk, your talk? I wouldn't say I remember the exact moment I realized I existed, but what I do remember is the moment I realized I stuttered.

"Shandice, it's your turn to read the next sentence."

As I anxiously sat on the floor, legs crossed, with my head looking up at the whiteboard, I prepared myself to begin reading. Each word I spoke was accompanied by a flutter my mouth was unable to deny. Surrounded by chuckling eight and nine year olds, I slowly attempted to release each word. But the simple sentence became a strenuous exercise I didn't have the strength to complete.

"Stop laughing, she is trying!"

I will never forget the fire in my year five Irish teacher's voice as she compassionately defended me while I tried my best to make it to the end of the sentence. She looked me sweetly in the eyes and attempted to soothe my discomfort with her smile.

It was at that moment I realized something was wrong with me. I felt barren when it came to producing sounds that would beautifully flow through the ears of others. Why couldn't my words bear fruit?

My sentences were strung together with umms and ahhs, long pauses, and a constructed belief that I was inadequate. I was shy, reserved, and a nervous speaker, fully aware of the untamed vibrations that left my mouth.

Words became my silent enemy, which I so desperately craved to be friends with. Why did my relationship with words have to be so complicated when I had so much to say? Why did I have to carry a defect I wanted to hide but would betray me every time I opened my mouth? I was burdened by my belief that because of how I spoke, I could never make a difference in the world. Too afraid to test my notion, my fears made a home in my deepest thoughts. That's when writing became my release, because, in my mind, speaking out loud was unconquerable territory.

19 |

Shine a light on your weaknesses—without worshipping their existence, so they no longer have the power to pull you down to your knees and into the darkness. Let them know that you are called to be a light.

20

Fear diminishes your faith and presents you with a lie.

I was always conscious of speaking in front of others in case what I said came out wrong. Avoiding that outcome at all costs, "It's better to say nothing than to sound like a fool, Shandice," I would coach myself out of having a voice, while open dialogue persisted in my mind.

My unhealthy relationship with words kept me on a strict diet of confinement, self-doubt, and self-pity. My voice became a symbol of inconvenience I didn't want to burden others with.

Lost in reverie, my mind became a breeding ground for unrealized dreams. I visualized myself speaking in front of millions of people who were captivated by my every word. Only God knows what I could have been saying for them to care, but, in my mind, I was a force to be reckoned with. In reality, my silence felt like shackles holding me back. I became a dreamer who didn't actually believe in what she was dreaming.

My year five teacher once said, "Shandice, darling, you will grow out of it." I was told it was only a phase, but the echoes of children laughing as I read out loud in class still haunt me today. Though my speech did eventually improve and I was no longer physically bound by my words, I was still mentally bound by the fragments they left behind. Ultimately, I grew out of my stutter and into a fear of speaking.

Terrified of echoing my past in new situations, I avoided conversations with others. I resisted confidently expressing my thoughts, ideas, and opinions. Always worrying that I'd make a mistake when I spoke. Overanalyzing my interactions with others—I grew up refraining from sharing my voice and confidently standing behind my words. I settled into the background, because I knew it was comfortable there, it was safe. Safe—but unfulfilling. My voice became my secret, but every now and then I would lend the world a sentence or two.

I remember being a child and wondering if my mum noticed. Wondering if she was embarrassed of me or thought I was broken and needed to be fixed. I struggled to figure out where I would ever go to be fixed, subconsciously carrying an internally crushing belief that I was never told to carry.

These thoughts began to corrupt my mind, beliefs not rooted in truth, but rooted in fear. The fear of being rejected for being imperfect and bearing weaknesses I had not yet fully understood.

Now looking through my adult eyes, I realize my mum was never embarrassed of me. She never made me feel unworthy, and she has never attempted to change me. Now I see: I was embarrassed of myself.

21

A beautiful mind isn't free from conflict, though darkness tries to consume its thoughts; light *always* wins.

So *freely* let it in.

22

It takes courage to walk through yourself and make it to the other side alive.

So let the fear fall from your eyes—you are feeling, you are healing.

23

Fear feeds off of inaction.

"Shandice, it's your turn to read the next page . . ."

My dislike for reading progressed from primary to secondary school. I would take a deep breath before beginning the first sentence, hoping to reach the end of the page without revealing my problem to the class. I would usually make it to the end just fine, nevertheless shaking with anxiety as I mumbled my way through each page. Every time I read without stuttering, I realized, "Hey, I can do this!" only to trip up and resist trying again.

"Ugh, I'm just a terrible speaker," I would whisper under my breath as I walked home from school. I painfully relived each and every human interaction, each and every class I had to read out loud or participate in. I even started researching careers I could quietly pursue that wouldn't require me to speak, but I was inevitably unsuccessful.

I had bullied myself out of having a voice, believing I had to measure up to the breathtaking communicators to whom I compared myself. I added insult to an injury that wasn't even my fault. And I didn't know how to nurse my mind back to health.

I was afraid of appearing as anything less than perfect—fearful of being rejected for being imperfectly me. Have you noticed that perfection in our minds is everything we are not? Causing us to worship what we admire in others while condemning ourselves into silent pain.

I rejected who I was in search of the person I wanted to be, unaware that the version of myself I dreamed of becoming lived in the woman I had fearfully denied. How much better would it be if we loved ourselves out of captivity, rather than tightened the chains with hate?

I had to make a decision: either build a new and healthy relationship with my words, one that would bear fruit, or continue digging through old weeds, reliving experiences that could no longer sustain the woman I was becoming.

24

Comparison kills uniqueness.

25

Sometimes I find myself stuck between the woman I once was and the woman I am becoming. Burning at both ends, afraid of turning to ash before sharing my light with the world. But then a voice within—so still and so certain—reminds me, "Darling, you are not stuck; your thinking is."

It's
time
to
take
your
power
back.

Upgrade your mindset, and stop thinking your freedom away.

26

We spend a lot of time running from the weapons of this world, often forgetting to disarm the weapons we've formed against ourselves.

Declare: I am ready to disarm the weapon of _____ that I positioned to destroy me.

27

Your self-talk should build you up, not break you down.

28

Fear hates it when you ask questions.

I had to ask myself, "Shandice, will your legacy be one of fear or one of courage? Will you stand up for your words through your actions? Or will you hide from your fears until you slowly disappear? Which one will it be? Which one will you surrender to?"

I became sick of being led by fear. So sick of deciding my fate based on my imperfections.

Why can't I be great by just being me?

Why can't I add light to the world by just. being. me?

I had to question my own authority. I was silencing my voice, and it was binding me up in a lie. I was slowly suffocating, but I had to be the one to believe my most authentic self was worthy of breathing freely.

I had put so much emphasis on my stutter that I couldn't locate the power that lived within me. I couldn't rest in the truth of those who courageously came before me and forged a path I can so freely walk down today. They did so much with so little because their vision was far greater than their circumstances, limitations, and differences.

So I turned my fears into words to memorize each and every time I felt lost in my insecurities. I wrote about how my maternal and paternal grandparents immigrated from Jamaica to

London in the '60s and built an incredible legacy that I cannot allow my insecurities to destroy. They didn't succumb to their struggles, *they always found a way through them.* They activated their God-given power and created a blueprint for me to embrace. Because of them, I am free to be whomever I desire. And when fear abruptly makes an appearance, attempting to burn my progress to ashes, I courageously recite over and over again, "You can't throw me into the fire and not expect me to rise."

29

Part of being a conqueror is knowing every downfall is the beginning of your uprise.

True victory is *overcoming*.

30 |

Every seed of fear that is rooted within you took time to grow there and will take time to root out. So be kind to yourself as you dig beneath old fears you once accepted—and courageously trust the timing of your process.

31

Your journey of discovery requires you to stick around long enough to uncover who you truly are, free from the world's perception of your being. So show up for yourself in the middle of your doubt, fear, and confusion. The fog will always fade if you are willing to patiently find what you are truly looking for.

32 |

Give your growing faith permission to override your doubts today.

33 |

The thing God gave you to liberate others will suffocate you if you don't release it.

34 |

Command your fears to the soles of your feet. Hasn't He given you the authority to trample on snakes and scorpions?

35 | 🌿

Fear is paralyzing until you touch courage.

If courage isn't the absence of fear, then strength cannot be the absence of weakness. I would ask myself, "When am I going to stop running away from my weaknesses? When am I going to challenge my perceived self? When am I going to face my fear . . . When?" But my questions continued to mount into a pile of failed attempts. I decided my fate was failure. I decided I had already lost the battle—until one day when I decided to touch courage.

***

Isn't it liberating when you step foot on territory you once thought was unconquerable? But still human, carrying weaknesses that cannot be overcome in a day. That's God, that's God working through you. I remember the first poem I read in front of a crowd, after writing my way through my late teens. It was the spring of 2010, and I was finishing up my study abroad year in the U.S. Just as I was preparing to return to London, I was introduced to a part of me I never knew existed.

I spontaneously signed up to be part of a talent show held on campus. I had discovered a love for poetry formed out of the thousands of words I had quietly penned in my journals. So I decided I would do the one thing I had talked myself out of doing for most of my adolescent life. I wanted to exercise my voice and share the words I felt rising from my chest, words that tapped on the shoulders of fear and prompted women and men alike to rise up and be free from the shackles their insecurities formed.

Still shaking, still scared, and still fighting the belief that I just couldn't do it, I spent countless nights writing and piecing together that poem. The writing turned into nights spent reciting each word over and over again. Recording myself on my laptop camera and playing those recordings over and over again. I had to do a great job. No, scratch that—I had to do *my* best job, I just had to. This poem was the longest poem I had ever written. It took me seven minutes to read every time and to this day, the line that rings in my ear is . . .

Pay attention to the things of this world you pay attention to, because without you even knowing, they are the very things molding you.

I had something to say, and for the first time I refused to hold myself back to bring forth any lies that could potentially hinder my progress. As I stood before the crowd, praying to God to fill my weaknesses with His strength, I took a deep breath, wiped my hands on my jeans to remove the sweat, and began reciting my poem.

I didn't umm and ahhh, nor did I stumble over my words. But that wasn't important, because I was standing on grounds I had never stood on before. As I introduced myself to the crowd, I also introduced myself to *me*. It was as if I was saying, "Hello, Shandice, nice to meet you. I am the Shandice who kicks a**." Ha, yeah. "I am the Shandice, who conquers her fears and doesn't believe everything she tells herself." I courageously spoke, something I wasn't used to doing. I gave myself a chance, a chance we often rob ourselves of because we're afraid of not delivering. Believing we cannot step up to the plate, forgetting who we serve.

Seven minutes later, I remember releasing my breath only to be breathing in the audience's applause. As sweet as their claps felt against my ears, the real substance of that moment was a renewed consciousness and understanding of myself that fear could no longer fool.

Little did I know that experience was teaching me a simple formula for no longer allowing my weaknesses to suffocate my desire to speak words of life and authentically be me.

I was within my reach—dreaming about her was no longer my only form of release.

I was introduced to purpose *in* motion and the courage required to answer the gentle call within, regardless of how much I questioned my own abilities.

Looking back, it's funny how you can *know* something to be true but still struggle to embrace that truth along the way. It hits in waves. Sometimes you surf that truth with courage, and other times you drown underneath the weight of being your most authentic self. And even though this painful battle secretly followed me throughout my twenties, I will never unlive the moment when I learned that when fear attacks your faith and presents you with a lie . . . don't flee, stand firm in truth, and *give that lie back.*

36 |

She always finds a way to use her broken pieces to rebuild her life.

She knows that pain has its purpose, and healing is a process.

37 |

There is no obstacle greater than your God-given ability
to overcome it.

38 |

Do you see the power that lives within you?

However tempting,

refrain from underestimating it.

Why? Because your source is *limitless.*

39

It takes time to become authentically you.

It takes intention to begin peeling back the layers and whole-heartedly embracing who God created you to be. The process hurts and breeds doubt at times, making you question, "Can I really do this?" But one thing I have learned is that courageous living requires courageous little steps. Each step breaks the lies, the false identities we sometimes adopt; *each step breaks the mold.*

Once the layers of comfort are gone, a beautiful canvas of truth remains. One you can begin to paint upon, guided by your inner light.

40 |

Your discomfort is purposely disconnecting you from who you *think* you are to powerfully connect you to the woman God created you to be.

You must first be uprooted
to then be replanted in truth.

41

God calls shy girls too.

As you build the confidence to be you, I want you to know
that you don't have to leap from one extreme to another. Start
by stripping the word *shy* from your identity and embrace the
woman you are called to be, *today*. There is nothing wrong
with being quiet and reserved and only choosing to speak
when you genuinely have something to say. Just do your best
not to shush yourself out of having a voice when your power
rises up inside you. Let it out and declare that *"shy"* will not
be your legacy.

42

To the quiet girls who want to live out loud.

You don't need to be the loudest in the room to be the *loudest* in the room. You can be gentle, vulnerable, soft-spoken, and still shake the room with your uniqueness.

43

Potential is a powerful seed, but it doesn't thrive inside us. It patiently waits for us to let it out, let it breathe, and develop into something greater. We often flirt with the idea of who we could be, rather than boldly become it.

44

To elevate to the next level, we must be willing to let go of the things holding us back. Elevating to the next level doesn't always mean a promotion—it can simply mean an elevation of thinking in preparation for what's to come.

45 |

The fruits of tomorrow live in the seeds of today. So water your seeds well. Don't allow fear to starve the core of the fruit you wish to bear.

46

One day, you will look back and be thankful that you didn't give up.
So continue to move with purpose.
Continue to dream above the ceiling.
Your faith can move mountains.

47

I used to always pray for God to put me in a place of influence where I could make a great difference in the lives of others.

Little did I know that in order for me to make the difference I desired, I'd have to go through things that would make me different. I'd have to go through uncomfortable seasons, trials that tested my faith, and pain that fractured my heart. I'd have to experience all the things I wanted to speak on, so my words weren't simply ideas. My words needed to represent the scars from the battles I'd won, not battles I'd run from—my words needed to be rooted in courage.

I had to learn how to use the weapons He had equipped me with and persevere to the end, even when giving up presented itself as a feasible option. So I no longer pray for influence. I pray for inner transformation.

I pray for guidance.

I pray for the confidence to wholeheartedly use the gifts I hold in my hands right now. To no longer wait for the perfect time or the perfect opportunity to serve those I am called to serve.

I pray for continued growth.

I pray for the perseverance necessary to stay rooted in truth and courage and not be swayed by the changing winds of this world. To no longer be led by emotion alone but for discernment and heavenly insight to revive my vision if I become jaded by the painful moments of life.

48

Prepare me for my purpose, Lord.

Prepare my heart to feel my purpose.

Prepare my eyes to see my gifts.

Prepare my mind to believe I'm worth it.

Prepare my spirit to truly live.

49

Have you noticed that the moment you know who you want to be in this world, it can become both a blessing and a curse?

You grip that idea of yourself so tightly that you rarely give it room to breathe. For the very first time, you dreamed beyond your natural threshold and met God in the clouds. Calling you to activate your wings and fly above the doubtful chatter in your mind.

I remember being a seventeen-year-old dreamer seeking a sense of purpose. I couldn't shake the feeling deep within that kept nudging me with a gentle whisper, "There must be more." But as a seventeen year old, what more could I want? I was getting good grades, making my own money working part-time in retail, and funding my weekend adventures. I had nothing to complain about—but I just couldn't shake the feeling that *there must be more.* I was searching for a mission that felt connected to my existence. Something that was bigger than me, not transient or fleeting, not dependent on grades or money. Instead, it depended on my willingness to access a part of myself I had not yet met by clearing the clutter that attempted to keep her hidden.

The feeling of *more* continued to strengthen as it yearned to be acknowledged, so I searched for its manifestation in books and found the possibilities to be quite pleasing.

Are you telling me I can make a difference by courageously being me? By uncovering my purpose and embracing it daily? I thought.

Yes! And *yes!* a steadfast voice replied.

Without any hesitation, I grabbed a pen and paper and began to write words that reflected my desired future and caused even my imagination to leap in faith. "I'll write books!" I wrote. "Somehow, someway, my words will free others, someday."

As I lay across my bedroom floor with papers scattered everywhere, I continued to pen my desired future, trusting the way would eventually be shown to me. And then that steadfast voice returned, greeting my core with the words, *You're right, there is more, and you are so much more than you currently see.*

***

However—the dream is just the beginning, and it's insane to think the very same mind that conceives it has the power to clip its wings before you've even lived it. There is work to be done, and more times than not, we are just too mentally young to understand the process of bringing a dream to life, to exist beyond our ego and external strife.

There is work to be done.

Both *inwardly* and *outwardly*.

The ability to strengthen your core so that you can carry the weight of your dreams as they begin to meet your reality is just as important as going out there and making them happen. Existing beyond your ego and external strife is realizing that you may fall down a few times along the way, but that doesn't make you a failure at life. It makes you a student of it. Slowly learning the ropes each day of an obstacle course you didn't create.

Things take time.

And just like a prematurely picked fruit doesn't taste that nice, you can't force-ripe your dream life. You have to be patient while doing your part, let the process *be,* and embrace it wholly.

50 |

Who you are becoming requires slow cooking, so don't be afraid of simmering a little. Embrace the process, thrive through the frustrating seasons, and actively cling to the promises of God.

51 |

How ironic it is that we can kill our dreams with the same mind that conceives them. So train your mind to nurture your dreams into reality instead of suffocating them.

The grave has enough dreams.

Your dreams deserve to live.

52

Feeling discomfort is not an indication that you cannot handle what's ahead. It's an indication that you will be stretched.

53

The process of being refined, stretched, and challenged—it's all necessary to grow.

Feel it.

Trust it.

Embrace its flow.

54

Three sacred lessons:

1. Every season holds the truth our ears need to hear. Pay attention.

2. Seek purposeful progression, not perfection.

3. Train for the mountain you desire to climb, but always be prepared to move mountains within.

55 |

Don't let anyone fool you into believing that what makes your soul jump isn't worth investing in. Even if that someone is *you*.

56 |

Fear said, "I just want to win, like her or like him."

Courage replied, "But the world needs to see you. Not a bootleg version of *them*."

It's time for everyone to meet the *real* you.

And even though you may not fully know what she looks or feels like, continue to do the inner work, so that you can meet her sooner rather than later.

***

All I've ever wanted to do is write books. To create a safe space for women to feel seen and heard and most importantly—be who they were created to be. To exist beyond their fears and doubts and break through the walls of their insecurities. But deep down, I never quite knew if *writing* was enough. I struggled to value my own voice, quietly doubting whether my words were worthy of being heard.

Valuing our voices is essential to releasing what truly lives within us. Seeing ourselves past our imperfections, quirks, and awkwardness while embracing the things that make us different is what truly sets us apart. If you cannot love and appreciate yourself as you grow through the different seasons of life, how can you expect anyone else to? We cannot sit in a dark room patiently waiting for someone else to choose us when we have the ability to choose ourselves first. We can no longer forsake our freedom for our fears or allow our misjudgment to lead the way. Nor can we put our insecurities on a pedestal and worship them like gods. Rather, we should lovingly accept the fact that we are forever growing and learning.

***

Give yourself permission to be present in your process of growth, release all you feel pulled to release—then watch it slowly multiply.

What God has placed within you is enough; *you* are enough. No extras needed.

57 |

No longer will I sit pretty, gift-wrapped with a shiny bow on top, never to be opened and fully used.

58

If you are cheating on your purpose with unfulfilling pursuits, I want you to know you deserve better. You were created for better, but you must be willing to *do* better.

59

You will always require courage to move forward.

Courage is not only needed to transition from a bad place to a good place; courage is also necessary to transition from a good place to a better place.

60 |

Sometimes *giving up* is an act of courage too.

So give yourself permission to change direction and embody the peace of authentic living.

61

There is no point persevering through something that is ultimately chipping away at your soul.

Focus on creating a deeper connection with yourself and your inner needs—so that you don't allow your goals to override your ability to reposition yourself as needed. With that being said, there is a difference between quitting for a cause and quitting because something is hard. After all, the hard things do stretch us further, but I don't believe in promoting a message that pushes us to suffer through experiences for the sake of appearing "strong."

62

Don't be afraid to say *no* to an opportunity that doesn't feel right for you. Just because it looks good doesn't mean it's good for you. We would all be better off if we chose purpose over pursuing a pathway backed by popular demand.

63 |

Everyone isn't passionate about the things you're passionate about. But that doesn't minimize the impact you can make on those who do care and need your service.

you are called and you have work to do

I am called to _____.

Grab your favorite coloring pens and use this space
to be a child again.

64 |

You are called, Dear Purposeful Woman. You are called, and you have work to do.

65 |

Lord, help me walk with confidence, knowing You sent me here to complete a purposeful mission.

66

You weren't created to be a clone of someone else. You were brought into existence to do what no one else could ever do. Individually purposed, not paired in twos. So resist the temptation of conforming to a world that's already overcrowded with copies.

Today and every day, *dare* to be you with courage.

67

No matter where you currently stand,

you can always make a difference.

So don't overthink the process.

Step one will lead you

> **to step two, and step two**

>> **will lead you to step three.**

Every stage of your journey is an opportunity to *give* and *grow*.

68

Timing is everything.

In your season of waiting, wholeheartedly believe and
prepare for the fulfillment of His promises.
Don't lose your vision to impatience and frustration.
Your time will come, and when it does . . . trust that you
are ready.

69 |

Believe in your vision, even when no one else does. You don't need their eyes to validate your sight.

70 |

I will not leave this earth without fulfilling my God-given destiny.

- I am faithfully finishing what I started.

- I am making a positive difference in the lives of those around me.

- I am learning my way through the ups and downs of life.

- I am courageously shining my light while leading the way with integrity.

71

When fear attempts to intimidate you and tell you that you can't, stare fear directly in the eye and tell it, "Oh, yes I can."

Don't forget who sent you.

Trust that you are a part of a victorious legacy.

72

Dear Purposeful Woman, "hard" does not mean "impossible" or "not meant to be."

73

Comfort is no longer in season.
Change cannot blossom there.

74

Opposition is an opportunity to test the fight within you.

75

Running in the opposite direction of adversity will only bring you to a place that doesn't reflect your best self. When challenges arise, don't flee; stay the course and conquer your trials with courage.

76

The good thing about hardship is that you don't have to sail alone.

God is always with you.

77

Temporary setbacks are just that: temporary.

I will not drown in the temporary.

I will persist and let this refining process lead me to my destiny.

78

You silenced your dreams out of fear that no one else was listening, but it's your ability to be true to yourself that awakens the truth in others.

79

I will no longer compress my dreams. I will expand my mind instead.

80

Shake off the fear, the doubt, and the belief that you're not good enough.

Shake off the whispers that you're too old, too young, too damaged, too shy.

Shake it all off.

Every single piece of it.

81 |

When you seek the one who created you, it's only a matter of time before you meet the real you. If you truly want to be you with courage, start by courageously seeking Him.

82

If I could send a message to the twenty-something-year-old me (fresh out of university and carrying a world of expectations on my shoulders), I would say:

"What looks like failure through the eyes of your shattered expectations is really the beginning of your making, your molding, your forming. The experiences you so desperately attempt to pray away are positioning you to carry the weight of your calling. You cannot bypass your refining path to walk in purpose. Just because it isn't paved in gold like you once thought it would be, doesn't mean the gold isn't waiting for you further down the road. But you mustn't give up. When things get tough or when you witness a superficial identity shedding from your soul, keep on shedding so that you can restore your roots with truth. Keep on shedding until you reach your core. You mustn't give up on yourself."

***

As I read these words again, I can't help but chuckle a little, because thirty-one-year-old me still needs to hear them. These words serve as a sobering reminder that everything I need is already within me. I think we all know the truth deep down but sometimes struggle to embrace it. It can be a struggle to take responsibility for your journey and surrender to the process. It can be a struggle to find the balance between your part and God's part; it often feels like an impossible balancing act of ifs, buts, and maybes. *Am I doing too much? Am I doing too little?*

The thing is . . . you will never really find the answer you're looking for unless you're willing to get your feet wet and explore the possibilities your present can produce.

But as a twenty-one-year-old fresh out of university, I lacked one key ingredient that threads this process together—*patience*. After graduating with a degree in marketing and TV production, I was so fixated on what I believed my present should look like that I was unwilling to embrace my unique process. Yet life has taught me that when we refuse to surrender to the process, we're often forced to release control so that we can discover something new about ourselves and the world around us.

I was determined to find a "prestigious" job in the marketing field so that I could save up enough money to return to the U.S. and get my master's degree within a year. I strategically studied marketing because I wanted to learn how to market myself and my books once I had become an author. Everything was so clear-cut and obstacle-free in my mind that I wasn't prepared for where my path would lead me.

After months of interviewing with one of America's top tech and consulting companies at a London-based office, I was let down by an email notifying me that they had over-hired graduates. This meant I had to go back to the drawing board and apply for more jobs. At this point, I had already missed the deadline for most graduate schemes in the U.K. and had little success with the ones that were open. So I ended up applying for a fundraising job, one of those positions with the highest of high turnover rates that would require me to stand on the streets of London and stop passersby for money. It didn't matter that I was the one who would literally sprint across the road to avoid those very people; now I was going to *be* one of those people . . . oh, the irony.

***

"I think you'd be perfect for this position!" said the young man sitting across from me as he offered me the fundraising job.

On the train ride to my very first shift in Chelsea, London, I found myself laughing over the fact that I was thirty minutes away from raising money on the streets for a charity called Guide Dogs for the Blind. *Me. Shandice. The shy girl who doesn't even like dogs. But I like people (for the most part), and I'd be making a difference, so how bad could it really be?* I thought.

The shift supervisor cheerfully greeted all the newbies. "Are you guys excited? Okay, you will need to be confident, enthusiastic, and not afraid to leave your comfort zone." I was certainly not the most confident, nor was I enthusiastic about my new position. After all, how confident and enthusiastic could I really be about the wave of rejection I was about to face?

I made it an hour into day two of the job when I walked up to my supervisor and said, "This isn't for me. I want to resign." He looked at me and replied, "You can do this, Shandice!"

I begged to differ. I was miserable. It was cold, it was embarrassing, and, honestly, it was all somewhat confusing. On my second day, I was traipsing along the streets of North London without a clue of how to ask random people for money. Then there was the rockstar-looking guy who approached me with some "advice" that didn't help either. "Maybe you should be bubblier?" he suggested.

I hadn't studied this in school, I wasn't passionate about this, and it didn't make sense to me.

"No, I want to go home. I'm sorry . . . I can't do this."

On the bus ride home, I contacted my old retail manager, Leanne, to see if she could possibly get me in contact with Sil, the manager at a local sports retail store near my house. I was desperate and had to put things into perspective; anything was better than that fundraising job.

Sil gave me the retail job without an interview. She knew I was one of Leanne's most valued staff members back when I worked there, so she was happy to take me on. For the first few weeks, I folded clothes, swept floors, and greeted customers. Not long after, she promoted me to the position of "Till Girl," putting me in charge of payments and refunds. I was cool with that, especially as the months grew colder (imagine if I were still traipsing around the streets of London fundraising!).

As thankful as I was for this job and the opportunity to make a living while I prepared for my next step, it took only a momentary encounter with a coworker to bring my deepest insecurities and fears to the surface. This fiery, tomboyish girl with beautifully curled ginger hair enthusiastically shared with me her plans for life after graduation. She was in her second year of university, studying psychology—filled with ambition and hopes for the future. But the moment she found out I had already graduated, she looked me dead in the eyes with her face scrunched up in disbelief and unapologetically said,

"I would *never* graduate and work at a retail shop."

My heart sank.

My mind sank.

I sank.

Shrinking smaller and smaller in embarrassment, I didn't know how to reply. She looked down on me, validating my deepest insecurities of being a "failure." And suddenly, I believed my temporary job description somehow determined my worth, my purpose, my destiny. Yet, deep down, I still wanted my life to represent the power of looking past my own sight and trusting in God's plan. In that moment, I was presented with the opportunity to wholeheartedly believe in something bigger than myself, despite my human understanding of where I currently stood. I had to believe that if I kept on walking and trusting, eventually, I would find my way.

83

Dear Purposeful Woman,

I know you question your position at times. You feel like you should be further by now based on a standard that was never meant for you.

But because you are working with God, I can confidently say that you are exactly where you're supposed to be.

So don't claim *their* standards or forfeit His plan when doubt sneaks up on you or when life gets messy. Instead, continue to stand tall in the truth of who you are.

And always remember to be you with courage along the way.

84

You are walking with a miracle worker.

So *walk* like it.

85

We expect our qualifications to open big doors for us; but when they don't, we easily give up, forgetting the key to our future has always lived within us.

86

Even when you convince yourself that your purpose is nowhere to be found, it **is** still there.

It is **in** you.

87

Plans change, positions change, but the essence of your purpose doesn't. So invest in the core of who you are instead of what life flaunts in your face.

88

God is training you for your purpose.

Though you ache from the movement of spiritual joints you never knew existed, continue to move them.

The pain you feel now is temporary.

Intermission

When I first decided to write this book, I had to commit to the humbling process of removing my ego from my art. I could no longer torture myself into birthing perfection, simply to prove a point. This project had to be an act of freedom—one where I could courageously unleash the woman I had attempted to neatly tuck away out of the fear of her not being "good enough."

I could no longer pack these words into boxes and archive them to collect dust just because they were written at a time when I was lost in the process of finding myself. I couldn't despise my words into secrecy any longer just because I was a young and inexperienced dreamer who wasn't fully prepared to step into her God-given identity.

I had to learn the sobering lesson that *purpose* trumps everything. It's not about making a debut, and it's not about being the brightest star in the sky. It's about realizing what you are here to release and releasing it until you take your very last earthly breath. *Vol. 1* represents me giving myself permission to evolve in my own unique way and be my most authentic self with courage. With every page and volume to come, I graciously invite you to uncover the beauty that lies in discovering *who* you truly are. For I want my words to spark a profound truth in you too.

At the beginning of this book, I invited you to use the empty spaces around my words to write your own because I don't want my words to serve as the ultimate guide for courage. Instead, I want them to serve as a gentle yet firm nudge to unleash your own voice and allow your God-given words to soak up your spirit. Even when you doubt whether your voice is worthy of being heard, always be the first to believe it is.

Stay true to the process,
Shandice from the present

89 |

Investigate who you authentically are instead of accepting the labels people assign to you.

You have to face yourself in the mirror, so focus on making *that* image clear.

90

Even when your surroundings look bleak, don't lose hope in the promises God whispered into the beat of your heart.

Instead,

steadfastly seek Him,

work according to your faith,

and prepare for the fulfillment of each promise.

Keep hope alive, drop your guard, and allow your heart to beat to His truth.

91 |

Get to know the Spirit that lives within you. Though absolutely gorgeous, you are more than your skin color, hair texture, and body. You are more than the school you attended, the car you drive, and the clothes you wear.

You are a Spirit filled with purpose.

And your flesh will continue to tremble in fear until it knows the Spirit that lives within you.

92

Lord, help us to be vehicles of Your truth.

Seeded.

Watered.

Saturated.

Rooted.

Intentionally maintained.

So much so,

purpose will have no choice

but to burst through our physical seams

and blossom.

93 |

If we truly take the time to understand the beauty and intention of rain, it will no longer have the power to drown us out of our destiny.

The storm will no longer be a hindrance;
it will be an opportunity to *grow*.

94

I wonder how many people miss their appointment with destiny by dwelling on the rain that was intended to nourish them . . .

95

"I'll be happy once I get my dream job."

"I'll be happy once I make 'X' amount of money."

"I'll be happy once I _____."

The truth is—you can claim your happiness right now. Life is way too short to wait for something you've always possessed.

You can leap for your dreams while appreciating the miracles that touch your life daily. So be careful not to miss out on the beauty of today while chasing an unpromised tomorrow.

96

We cannot deny that this human life of ours holds many complexities. A spinning wheel that starts and stops and thrills us with hopes and laughter. But sometimes it falls flat and hits us with unknown sorrow. And when that sorrow scarily stares us straight in the face, remember: happiness is a state we *choose*, not a destination we endlessly chase.

97

Gratefulness is consciousness.

When I consciously acknowledge, in the midst of my trials, that I still have a lot to be grateful for, the mountains in my mind begin to move. Temporary, external conditions no longer hold the power to cloud my ability to see the light that radiates through my life. I am free to bask in the sun's bliss and smell the roses of a summer's day. Though storms may appear some nights, my joy is here to stay.

(Overcoming has always started within.)

98

Needless to say, I didn't last long at the retail shop. As much as I tried to pretend, my ego was bruised. I couldn't get the encounter with the fiery, tomboyish girl (with beautifully curled ginger hair) out of my head. And when the next opportunity presented itself, I went for it.

In the spring of 2012, I applied for a sales advisor desk position working for a coach company and landed a group interview.

"Attention, candidates! I would like to make something clear to you all. Many of you may not be aware of the ins and outs of this position, so I'd like to explain a few details before we go any further," said a middle-aged man dressed in a grey, tailored suit. Squinting my eyes with confusion, I scanned his persona. "This position will not be in a cozy little ticket office," he continued. "You will not be selling tickets through a window behind a desk. Instead, you will be selling tickets outside on the pavement, sometimes in the cold. You will be working a combination of day and night shifts. The weather can get pretty bad through the night, so if you don't feel up to it, I am giving you the opportunity to leave now."

My body tensed up in disbelief. My mind was screaming, *Go, Shandice! Run, run! Run for your life!* But with not a single other person making a run for it, I just sank deeper into my seat.

***

A few days after the interview, I received a voice message saying, "Hello, Shandice. This is Trevor from the coach company. Can you please get in contact with me at your earliest convenience? I would love to talk to you regarding your interview."

It was him—the grey-suited man from the interview—and he sounded like he had good news to deliver.

***

Like most interviewees, I was asked, "Why do you want to work for us?"

Good question! I thought before responding with, "Well, I enjoy working in customer service roles." LIES. "I also want to gain more experience working in an environment that will challenge me to grow." More LIES. For better or worse, I couldn't stop myself from telling a made-up story that was soothing to the ears. Once I got the hang of it, I was an expert at explaining why I wanted to work outside in the cold in the early hours of the morning to make a living.

***

When I gave Trevor a call back, he enthusiastically offered me the position.

"I'd love to take the job!" I said. By this point, the lies continued to drop from my tongue.

"Fantastic!" he replied.

I tensed up with both excitement and dismay. *What have I actually gotten myself into?* I wondered.

***

One 3:00 a.m. alarm, two bus rides, and six layers of clothing later, I was selling coach tickets at an outdoor bus stop in bitterly cold London for eight hours a day. My position was a far cry from what I believed my purpose would produce, and not a day passed by that I didn't feel embarrassed for not being further ahead, for being a woman in transition, for having dreams I had yet to birth. Through my eyes, purpose had left my side, and I no longer knew how to grasp it.

I remember the day I left work early because I felt like rubbish *once again*. I walked through the front door of my mum's house and fell into her arms in tears. As she held me tightly, trying to figure out what was wrong, I whispered, "I failed myself." As those words left my mouth, I sank deeper into her arms, bawling my eyes out.

My mum held me tighter and spoke out to God, "I didn't send my one daughter to university to be selling tickets at a bus stop."

I knew her words were not an attack. They were her way of simply saying, "I want better for you." And I couldn't fault her. I wanted better for myself.

***

After my meltdown, I went into my bedroom to hide underneath my covers and continue my pity party. A few hours later, God placed six simple words in my heart that totally rocked my world . . .

"Do you know who you are?"

I quickly jumped to my own defense, "Of course I do! I'm Shandice, a twenty-three year old with a degree in marketing and TV production." It wasn't until after I blurted out my response that I realized I hadn't answered His question. God was asking me if I knew who I was beneath the titles, qualifications, and all the other ego-boosters I had attached to my self-worth.

I couldn't answer, because I had allowed my job description to become my identity. I dismissed the fact I had a purpose that broke through the walls of my 9 to 5 (or 3 to 11), and that I could walk in purpose at any given moment regardless of my circumstances.

A few hours later, my mum came to check up on me. Peeping her head through my bedroom door, she said, "You know your purpose and your profession are not the same thing, right?" She wanted me to know I had nothing to be ashamed of. When I explained to her that I felt like my job was holding me back from my purpose, she left me with words that opened my heart in a whole new way.

She wanted me to know that jobs change, but the essence of your purpose doesn't. It's yours. It's within you. It is not something to place on a pedestal so far outside your reach that you only take external steps to get there.

She was right. This job was temporary. It had an expiration date, and it was not *my* end. In fact, it was somewhat of my beginning. But somewhere along the line, I had gotten stuck in an identity crisis.

I thought I knew who I was based on where I was, but God was prompting me to look deeper. He wanted me to see myself the way He sees me and base my worth in Him, not my temporary position. My eyes were opened to the reality that if I continued on that path, I would end up going through life like a roller-coaster ride—up when things looked good and down when they didn't mirror my distorted image of success.

***

I had to start peeling back the layers and think seriously about who I was created to be. I had to embrace the steps and take heed of how they mold, sculpt, and refine us. They prepare women with big dreams to do big things by teaching us to embrace small beginnings. Imagine how much more we would enjoy the journey if we simply appreciated the steps rather than despising the brief stops that prepare us to live and breathe the life we've always dreamed of. Experience is a powerful tool; it's greater than any qualification given by man. Testing, trying, failing, and getting back up teach us more than sitting in a classroom and taking an exam ever could.

You see, I needed that job to ground me in truth. I needed my sales advisor position to remind me that one chapter doesn't get to define my whole story. I couldn't forget the promises God had spoken over me. I couldn't forget that voice that confirmed my quest for more; there was more in me. *So much more.* But for a moment, I let my job description stand in the way of my true identity.

My greatest lesson within that season of my life was that my job description does not determine my destiny. If you find yourself in a similar position, I hope you stamp this truth across your heart. I am so much more than I could physically see at the time, but I allowed the material world to clothe me in an identity that was never meant to own me. And I have one thing to say about this battle that claims so many of our lives as we struggle to find ourselves solely in what we do:

In all seasons, shine your light unapologetically bright. Start training your mind to love the most authentic version of yourself, so when the world attempts to dress you with their lies and fears, you can reject them without feeling naked.

99 |

Look no further.

Your existence and purpose have already been approved by God.

100

At this very moment, you are still precious, usable in God's eyes, and created for a purpose.

101

Declare:

Approval isn't something I need.

It isn't something I seek.

Purpose doesn't need approval.

102

Watch the words you take in.

I have learned not to digest the empty opinions of others. They take up internal space, only to leave you unfulfilled and drained in the long run. If someone's opinion about your life holds no real substance, *release it* and keep it moving.

It's time to tune out the naysayers and tune in to your higher calling.

103

Every pause along your journey is necessary for preparing you to become the woman God created you to be. Embrace the **stillness** as much as you embrace the *movement*.

104

Even in your loneliest, most painful moments, purpose is always by your side.

105

Wherever God takes you, He will keep you.
Through every transition you face, He is here.
Through every obstacle, He is here.
Do not fret, Dear Purposeful Woman, He will not
abandon the work He has started within you.

He is always here.

106

The world is not your assignment giver, so I urge you to silence that voice that comes to steal you away from your purpose.

107

You are a product of the same God who rose Jesus from the cross. Now tell me what you cannot rise from?

108

When I don't know what to pray for, help me, Lord, to come before You and trust my needs will be met.

109

Even though the rainbow delights our eyes, the rain nourishes our soul. Embrace *all* seasons.

110

I am *still here* for a purpose.

111

In the midst of our busy lives, it's important we take the time to stand still and focus. It's what brings life into perspective; it lights up what matters, dims what doesn't, and orders our eyes to stay centered in truth.

112

In case you ever wondered, not even the ceiling can hold your dreams.

keep your head up

113

If Jesus can conquer the cross, you can conquer your day.
Keep your head up, Dear Purposeful Woman.

No need to carry the stresses of tomorrow.
Take it one day and one step at a time.

One step, two step, three step, four.

114

You'll get so much more done today if you free yourself from unrealistic expectations. An overwhelmed spirit will have to fight so much harder to overcome.

Drop
the
heavy
load.

115

Distinguish the difference between busyness and productivity. Drop the extra baggage and pick up peace and contentment. Busyness is not a prerequisite for success in any area of your life. So slow down when need be,

and . . .

breathe.

116

Break the mold the world so fearfully created for you as a result of their own fears. Break it by *shaking* the norm.

117

I will not allow anyone to validate what they didn't create.

118

You have nothing to prove.

In a world obsessed with oversharing, save some things for you.

119

Your emotional, mental, and spiritual space is valuable.
So pay close attention to what you allow inside your temple.
Be careful not to consume too much of anything that leaves
you feeling drained and disconnected, especially in the
high-volume social media world we live in. Practice the art of
building your own community (*online and off*) through purposefully choosing who and what you follow and give attention to.
Freely audit what you are allowing *in*; you reserve the right to
keep anything that harms you *out*.

120

Remove the noise.

The extra stuff.

The extra people.

The extra fluff.

All the extras that add nothing extra to your life.

Quality is a jewel we often exchange for quantity, but less can indeed create space for more.

121

Every time I have stepped out in faith, the ground beneath my feet has been stronger than I could have ever anticipated. For when we leap, we eventually land on solid, unshakeable ground.

So leap, Dear Purposeful Woman, and *be you with courage* along the way.

122

Let's live beyond the ceilings we create for ourselves out of the fear we cannot break through them.

Let's fly higher than we contemplate our wings can carry us.

Let's defy the rules of society and prove that we are not bound by the expectations, statistics, prejudices, or small minds that attempt to minimize our greatness.

Let's live what many deem as the impossible.

123

The words God spoke to you
were intended for you.
So don't give them back to Him out of fear.
They are yours.

Yours to **own.**
Yours to **keep.**
Yours to **live by.**

So live by them—as only you can.

124

There have been times when God would speak to my heart, and instead of embracing His word, I became an expert at giving it back to Him.

If He wrote me a letter and addressed me by name, I'd still probably doubt whether it was even God's handwriting.

But doesn't the Bible say, "My sheep know my voice"?

The thing is, it's easy to lose God's voice in the midst of the world's noise, especially when you are not seeking it out. We've created a world where we celebrate the mini-god within us all, forgetting that it's the God *in* us that should be glorified— *not us*. But when the applause starts and loudens, it only gets harder to redirect it. So instead, we start questioning if being a sheep in Christ's flock is even worth it.

My faith has increasingly become a struggle, not because I don't believe, but because I am wrestling with how this world presents my faith. *It's messy.* Constantly counterfeited and manipulated to suit selfish agendas. My faith feels so misunderstood, even by me at times. It feels tainted, malleable, and unobtainable.

I despise what this world has done to my faith.

And maybe that's an oxymoron because "my faith" is just that—mine.

Is it really worth fighting with the world for what is already mine to purposefully pour into and nurture?

Is it really worth fighting with God over how others choose to represent Him?

And is it really worth angrily judging the actions of others as I struggle to pick up the pieces of my beliefs and rebuild something solid?

Maybe the answer is simply to keep my stones to myself and instead use them to build an internal kingdom where His presence can reside and guide me to *my* freedom. I'm still in search of the answers here, but I'm no longer afraid to ask the questions. And if there is anything I know for sure, it's that I can no longer reject the words God has spoken over me because I fear being part of a faith that's *messy*.

125

I will not allow God's legitimacy to be defined or polluted by those who have hurt me over the years. I will not allow God's fullness to be determined by human brokenness.

126

Choosing to walk in faith and trust the God you claim to believe in while intentionally doing the inner work to cultivate childlike faith is difficult; sometimes, you inevitably get hurt along the way.

There's a residual effect of shattered expectations. The ones that crushed our core and stuck around throughout our childhood and early adult years. They taught us how to be afraid of what we dreamed. They taught us to be wary of our fleeting realities, giving them far more power than they deserved.

I learned pretty early on how to fear my dreams and the idea of living them out loud. From this fear, I developed a distaste for abundantly living out all that God had promised me, because I was no longer a dreamer who believed in the impossible. Instead, I became a skeptic who believed I was undeserving of what I once knew was already mine.

Even through all of life's trials and tribulations, I have always carried the sentiment that no matter how hard life gets, I will not allow it to harden me. And as cute as that sounds, my softness often feels like a curse. Vulnerability, openness, and childlike faith all sound like things I should run from; they require me to surrender to the notion that no matter how old I get or how much power I acquire, I'm still a fragile human being in the end. And although there is so much more to all of us than flesh, blood, and bone, it's undeniable that our tiny bodies can break into a thousand pieces at any moment in time, erasing our physical existence in a flash.

. . . and that terrifies me more than I'd like to admit.

So I sit down and have conversations with God. I ask Him, "Why am I even here, and what is the point of it all? The fact that I can be here today and gone tomorrow. The fact that people can break my heart and I can fall apart. The fact that I'm navigating a world filled with brokenness, pain, and sin. Why am I even here, and what is the point of it all?"

For when our futures become tainted by the thought of disappointment, doubt begins to seep in. And before we know it, we no longer believe in the things we once did, so we shy away from making bold moves. Why? Because we no longer view the world through innocent eyes.

And then I think about God calling us to have childlike faith and restore the eyes of a child when we are an adult who has gone through stuff. I am propelled to start altering the way I perceive my experiences so that they can no longer bruise my core and feed me lies. I want to be wise, but I always want to be free to see things in a way that human wisdom cannot comprehend. I no longer want to be practical or rational; I want to be spiritual and liftable. I want my wings to show themselves in moments that I don't feel strong enough to fly. I can no longer be held bound by this physical form; I know it is weak, but it isn't all that I have.

***

As I walked through my mid-twenties, my childlike faith was on life support, waiting for a revelation to revive it. I saw, felt, and heard God every day, but I didn't know if I could trust Him. My understanding of His love was tangled up in worldly distractions. I continued bearing witness to men and women who claimed to house the Spirit of God while spewing hate and judgement towards His children in ways my soul couldn't justify, even through the mind of an innocent child. I saw pastors take advantage of their congregations, using their insecurities and fears to further bind them up in lies. I witnessed idol worship and inequality—left, right, and center. And as I did my best to hold onto the eyes of a child, I failed at every corner. I knew I had to restore my faith in God even though I struggled to understand how His name had been pimped out for the glory of man, with justice yet to be served.

At that moment in time, I had two options: pull the plug on my faith, or be patient with it. I chose the latter. I chose to sit by the bedside of my spirit and keep feeding it truth until I was strong enough to breathe on my own without inhaling the hurt of this world. I chose to use it as fuel to spread truth and help restore the innocent eyes of other women so that together we could all regain our wings and fly to freedom.

And while it has taken me some time to heal and regain my vision, I refuse to let the world steal my innocent eyes. It may take some time to heal them, but, no, world, you cannot have them.

127

She found her wings hidden beneath her misconception of flying. Before her discovery, she thought aiming too high would only leave her disappointed in the end. So she ignored the origin of her limbs, reaching only for what she deemed possible to grasp.

But the wind refused to let her wings retire before experiencing their might.

At first, she refused to surrender, frustrated by the tug of war. But as the ground-level began taking a toll on her frame, the wind began to rage, declining her plea to settle down.

And then she heard a steadfast voice, prompting her to rise and fly.

So, for the very first time, she rose, and she flew. And when she reached an unfamiliar place, the wind continued to rage, but its presence felt different from above. Tapping on her shoulder, it whispered one, simple word—*fall*. And it was at that moment that her wings were made known to be the assistance God granted her to soar through the skies of life. To fly high, touch her purpose, and make it known to those still afraid to fly that they, too, house wings beneath their misconception of flying.

We must be willing to *fall* if we dare to fly high.

128

Fly high so you can practice the art of trusting God even when you fear His abandonment.

Let Him show you He isn't like man. Let Him show you He will not retract His promises. Let Him show you the reason He placed gifts, visions, and wonder within you. Don't let fear seduce you into keeping your wings neatly tucked away, never to experience what it's like to rise and fly.

May you always embody the courage to use those beautiful, mighty wings of yours.

129

Oh, God, you have never stopped pursuing me.

130

"Wanna go to church with me?" asked my school friend Manny.

I got dressed for church that Sunday morning like I was meeting God for the very first time.

Though He had been a constant companion in my life, His depiction in previous religious settings had caused me to question His essence based on how others portrayed Him.

One experience in particular comes to mind. I was fourteen years old and visiting a friend's church in East London when our youth group was lined up and told not to move until we spoke in tongues. If we didn't know how, we were led to believe God's Spirit was far from us.

It was at that moment I learned what religion was and how God didn't live in that place.

Though I had yet to find where God lived, I knew He wasn't an author of confusion. I knew He was a gentleman who pursued us in His own special way.

After attending that church for a little over a year, I secretly withdrew from my faith. I still believed in God, but I couldn't get behind the God they created in the four walls of that church. So when Manny invited me to attend his church, though I was skeptical at first, I felt enough time had passed for me to reopen my heart. I was ready to surrender to a new process of building community, learn more about God in a church setting, and rebuild the trust I had lost in my tender early teens.

While I don't recall the specifics of the service that day, I do remember finally feeling at peace. The kind of peace that reminded me that, underneath it all, *God is real.* God is love. And the life of Jesus is one I should get to know like the back of my hand, so that if another situation should attempt to contain my faith, I'd have a reference point of truth and love I could surrender to.

***

The fear of beginning a new faith journey at seventeen was still very real. I knew this journey would require me to open up and go deeper than I had ever gone before. So I did what my seventeen-year-old self knew to do. I made an opening but refused to expand it. "Let's stay on the surface for now," I said.

As a woman who identifies as a Christian, a believer, and a woman of God, I must keep it real. My freedom doesn't live in those terms or titles. Freedom opened its arms to me the moment I realized I was simply *His*—created by God for His purpose. I can sing the songs, lift my hands up high, and quote you every scripture in the Bible, but if I cannot stand before Him with a heart cultivated by His grace, love, and conviction, I am nothing but a decorated vessel yet to be saturated by His truth.

God is for all to see, hear, feel, and experience, and He has shown me that He ultimately reigns above the boxes we often create for Him.

So I give my life to Him, not your traditions.
I give my life to Him, not your political party.
I give my life to Him, not your idea of who He is.

I am His.

So I give my life to Him.

131

I will not allow anyone to put my
faith in their box.
The God I serve is not six-sided.
He is infinite.

132

Artificial food won't sustain you for a kingdom journey.
Seek His daily bread.

133

Whatever boundaries you need to set to keep a sound mind and flourish, do it. You will thank yourself later.

Guard your heart and mind.

134

You are under no obligation to fellowship with negativity.

Protect your spirit.

135

Forgive me, Lord,

for the times I have spoken hastily against myself and others.

May my words reflect Your love and grace daily.

May my words promote Your peace and purpose always.

Sometimes our words start wars that we never dreamed of starting, when, deep down, we so desperately crave to heal our already open wounds.

136

Your peace is awaiting your permission.

137

You are not behind.

You are not obligated to pursue a path you feel no real connection to. Let go of that belief and pick up the specific duties, talents, gifts, and skills that God has placed in you to be nurtured.

You don't need to fear never being seen. You don't have to restrict yourself to only showing the parts of you that you believe will be accepted—only doing the work that you believe will be applauded while ignoring the truest tug at your heart.

Start listening to your spirit instead. Start hearing God's voice. Start paying attention to what your current reality is slowly revealing to you.

You don't need to decorate your purpose to be more appealing or palatable. Resist getting caught up in presentation rather than substance and depth. Presentation is important, but you have to ask yourself, "Am I trying to present who I authentically am, or am I trying to present something popular to appeal to the public's wandering eyes?" I truly believe, whatever you do, you should do it with heart, or it cannot pump life into others. Do it like you mean it. Get to know your why and use it as fuel so that you can go the distance even when you don't *feel* up to it.

I had to remind myself that, as much as I wanted to be prepared and polished, my purpose is not a marketing strategy, a brand style guide, or color palette. My purpose is a part of His master plan, and I must first and foremost partner with God.

If you are struggling to walk with purpose, take a step back. Give yourself permission to detach for a few days, weeks, or even months so that you can detox from the unnecessary expectations you've placed on yourself. And as you detach from all the pressure, start attaching yourself to truth. Make room to intently tune into God's voice so that you can slowly but surely find your way back home to your most authentic self, a place where purpose freely resides.

138

Ambition isn't enough.

Why?

Because we all want to reach
the top of the mountain.
But the question remains:
Why are you climbing?

139

Turn your painful lessons into meaningful gems you share with others—rather than harmful stones you throw at yourself.

140

In the blink of an eye, so much time has passed, and it's easy to doubt whether or not you have made progress.

Memory loss is not only experienced by the elderly; those of us who are physically young can often forget the battles won and focus on the goals yet to be accomplished. We can be so eager and bold with our pursuits yet fragile in the face of disappointment. We carry good intentions without understanding that the journey is calling for more than just good intentions; it is calling for honesty, patience, and perseverance. Your inner self needs to know that you will not bail when you begin to unravel in the face of hardship.

You must be willing to sail and part the sea with deep faith, despite what others say along the way. Oh, how the words of those who turned back too soon echo louder as you make your way past what they were too afraid to finish. Those words attempt to outstay their welcome and remodel your mind as you make your way through the valley. But you mustn't become accustomed to voices that cannot awaken truth in you. Learn to tune them out; better yet, stay clear from their chatter.

But the question still remains: What do you do when the chatter is internal? Though you have defeated the voice once or twice, it comes back with a vengeance, ready to devour your progress.

There are seasons in our lives when we feel like everything is falling apart. All the while, those seasons are laying the foundation for exponential growth and opportunities; those seasons reveal a power we never quite knew existed within us, a power that patiently awaited its turn to exist *through* us.

***

I didn't always allow myself the time and space necessary to mature through each season of my life, and I always expected more from myself than I had the capacity to give. I was attempting to rush a journey that craved to be honored and valued as an important part of the refinement process. It's easy to believe you are behind when you look around and see so many other people doing what you have spent the majority of your life dreaming about. What we often forget is that they, too, are on a journey, and we don't know how their path started or where they currently stand. We see the fruit of watered seeds without knowing their timelines, their ups, or their downs. We are witnesses of their success but not insiders to their process.

When you place a ticking clock over your process, it becomes easy to overwater your seeds to force their growth, drowning your potential, all in the name of feeling behind or feeling like a failure. The need to rush will have you accepting any and every opportunity to feel valued and successful for a temporary moment rather than embracing the days of small beginnings and allowing the sun to slowly shine on what you are forming beneath the ground.

Your process is yours. Your journey is yours. And though you have the freedom to share it with the world, share it for the right reason, not to simply prove a point and let it be known that you too are working. I have found that the most powerful moments along my journey were often undocumented and uncaptured. They were supernatural moments, gifts from heaven that I simply couldn't plan for or catch on camera. So as you continue to move through the world, know that your progress is still meaningful. Whether you feel seen or unseen, you are always seen by God.

141

You will have to rise above their expectations and limitations. You will have to stand by your *yes* even when they shout *no*. And above all, you will have to rise above your own limitations birthed out of your own disappointments. Even when life lets you down, you still have what it takes to rise back up.

142 | 🌿

Rising above my own expectations meant I had to be willing to trust my unique process and believe that with time, faith, work, and God's guidance, I would eventually find my way and bear witness to all I had once envisioned.

I also had to realize that the seemingly wasted parts of my journey and the seasons that challenged me beyond my natural threshold were all necessary for me to get to this very moment in time. I had to reach the point where I could transcribe my words from a place of deep acceptance and appreciation for my journey thus far, no longer despising the process that birthed this present moment.

So as I lie across my bed, writing the final pages of a book I have dreamed of since I was seventeen years old, I am reminded of the jobs that taught me not to place my value in fleeting things, titles, or forever-changing descriptions. I am reminded of the tender, hopeful young woman I once was and how often I placed her in a box, waiting patiently for the perfect time for her to be seen and accepted. And as I write these final words, I wonder if maybe God was the one hiding me. Maybe He created a sacred place for me to be molded and refined so that when the moment came for me to finally release my words into the world, I could do it from a place of true freedom, not obligation or fear. Maybe all my past failed attempts were really Him protecting me from myself, teaching me the art of patience and perseverance, while giving me an opportunity to live and breathe the words released in the "messy middle."

Let's talk about that—the messy middle. The in-between that feels oh-so-confusing at times. The place that often throws mud on our masks and dares us to take them off. It challenges us to dig beneath the surface of our thoughts and believe in something bigger, something lasting and sacred.

The messy middle is the place where we slowly unravel and remove the knots that once held us bound as we go out into the world and discover things about ourselves that only life experiences could reveal. It is the place our hearts get broken and mended as our spirits get tested and strengthened. A place filled with so much hope and wonder, even though the process can be painful.

So as you gather words from the pages of this book, I hope this is one of those pages you never forget. I hope you hold onto the truth that your identity runs deeper than where you currently stand. The moment you give yourself permission to embrace your messy middle is the moment you'll create an opening to navigate life with purpose and courage—no matter what each season brings.

At the time, I didn't realize my life was writing the story I would one day have the courage to tell. I was so busy trying to justify my vision in real-time that I often lost sight of the beautiful process unfolding before my eyes. But, as I shared earlier in this book, there is no time for regret; there is only gratefulness for the lessons and blessings we have the opportunity of learning.

Even though I have experienced so many internal struggles, when I pause and reflect, I flash back to the moments when I used my struggles to fuel my journey. They remind me that I am capable and all things are possible for those who believe.

***

In the summer of 2019, a few months before my thirtieth birthday, I had been seeking God regarding my writing and my direction in general. Throughout every stage of my twenties, I always questioned if I should have had a book published by that point. I couldn't help but wonder if there was something wrong with me for taking "so long." I placed so much unnecessary pressure on myself, unaware of the work that was taking place within me.

On that summer night, I was in my hotel room in Atlanta, Georgia, on a business trip (a far cry from my bus stop days). And though I now had a "good job" and a "good life," I couldn't deny this nudge in my spirit that maybe it was the right time to finish my first book. With a box filled with pages of words spanning over twelve years, I prayed to God that each word would be used for good. I needed to give the woman in my twenties a voice before I could move on and release the Shandice I knew I was becoming. I couldn't grow past this season without shedding light on what has made me who I am today.

So that night I prayed to God to give me a sign. I prayed He would speak to me about my writing, because, as strong as the feeling was, I still doubted the pull within.

The very next morning I got up and got ready for my work meeting. Seated at the front of the room, I was tasked with leading the marketing strategy portion of each business session. During one of the sessions that didn't require my input, I noticed a LinkedIn notification on my phone. I saw a connection request and message that read:

Afternoon Shandice,

I read your blog this morning, 'A Prayer For Grace in Frustrating Situations.' It really spoke into my current situation and also helped members of a small group. Because of that prayer, I was able to walk out of my house in peace.

You clearly have a gift.

Thank you.
Chris
Keep being you.

Stunned by the moment, I couldn't release my breath. I clicked on his profile, only to find out he was based in London—my city, my home. Tears began to cloud my eyes, so I wiped them quickly to avoid any of my team noticing.

How ironic, I thought to myself, *that my sign came all the way from London.* The very place my journey began. From a guy I have never met. A guy who, out of the blue, found my blog when he needed words to meet him where he was and get him out the door.

***

It's funny how God used us both to help one another; we were vessels for His glory. Like I said before, **that** is purpose in its purest form—simply being a light and sharing it in any way you can. In that moment, there were so many voices around the room contributing to my work meeting, but I couldn't hear a thing. I was deeply in tune with God's glory, to the point of no return.

I finally felt the nudge I had been waiting for to just do this! I had to stop resisting the path I truly wanted to go down once and for all. At that very moment, I declared to myself, *I can't turn back. I have to do this.* And I knew that until I got over the first hump, I would always find an excuse to turn back. So I picked up my box (filled with pages of words that have become this book) and a pen and got to work. And just like that, the book I so desperately wanted to write began to write itself.

143

So many of us aren't birthing our God-given vision because we are lying back and waiting for things to magically happen.

It's time to get up and *move* mountains.

144

Jesus didn't die on the cross for you to be crucified by your fears time and time again.

145

Stand up for what you believe in.

No one on this green earth deserves the power to dictate your pathway.

What direction is your spirit calling you towards?

For the approval of man means nothing without the approval of God.

146

Oh, how God does wonders with willing hearts.

147

Hold onto the pep in your step—your spark, your smile, the thing that sets you apart.

Keep it close

and *multiply it.*

148

Declare: Things are looking up, and I'm not going to settle for less.

Train your mind to speak and embrace the reality you desire, not the false reality you fear.

149

I am a woman of completion. I finish what I start. I do what I say I'll do.

150

Don't underestimate the power of sticking with God. Things may not always happen on your watch, but the beauty of God's timing never fails.

151

When you know who you are, you will surpass the world's expectations or lack thereof. You will surpass the negativity, false labels, and family patterns. You will excel in truth and purpose as the woman God created you to be.

152 | 🌿

You are worthy of it all. But you must believe you were truly made for this.

You are worthy of the highs, and you are capable of overcoming the lows. God took His time when making you. You were not simply dropped into this world; you were birthed, and you were purposefully placed into a scene created to tell a story of His redemptive love—a story where you are *free*.

A story where you are not accustomed to being a stranger to yourself. A story where you don't shut yourself down out of fear of what you could find if you dig deeper. A story about meeting yourself wherever you are along your journey.

I didn't always embrace my truest self. I felt her presence but never took the time to unwrap her. I carried her dreams but never traveled through her mind to locate where those dreams were conceived. *I didn't know her. But I judged her.* I judged her imperfections. I judged her tendencies to run and hide in fear behind the image she created for herself. An image that was conflict-free, one that complimented the picture our society often tries to paint for us. Until you courageously pick up a brush, decide to embrace your intricacies—even when no one else does. You choose to awaken the truth, and you put the lies to sleep.

153

I once thought there would be this *feeling* of courage that would consume me to the point of no return. My fears would disappear; my worries would collapse; my doubts would fade away. The truth is, courage only runs through our veins when we decide to move and face the unknown. It is activated by our decisions—both internal and external. Not by staying in one place, waiting for the feeling to magically appear.

When we decide to do the things that scare us and make us feel uncomfortable, courage shows up in unconventional ways to remind us that we are equipped for the journey ahead. Even when we are afraid and don't feel like we can do it; faith has the power to open our eyes to a new world of possibilities.

So before you throw that mustard seed away because it appears too small and insignificant, remember what Jesus said: "You will say to this mountain, 'Move from here to there,' and it will move, and nothing will be impossible for you."

154

I won't go back,
for I am in tune with He who calls me forward.

155

It takes commitment, dedication, and an unshakable belief that you are not only here for a reason, but that reason will not die with you. That reason will no longer remain your secret; it will become your mission, your blueprint . . . your life's work. You will no longer reserve dreaming for your lunch breaks or when you see someone else accomplishing their goals. You will dream through your actions; you will work harder than you dream. You will wholeheartedly embrace the process of becoming a dreamer who works.

156

We think too much about it,

talk too much about it,

dream too much about it.

We should pray more,

trust God more,

go for it more.

Become a dreamer that *lives* it.

157

Things are changing.

Fear doesn't have the same effect on me as it once did.

I still feel it, but it can no longer bind me.

I still hear it, but it can no longer drown out the voice of God.

Courage has my ear now.

158

And you, darling, are the head and not the tail; you are above your fears and not beneath them. So keep your head up and courageously flourish with *purpose*.

159

Take a moment to appreciate the mountains your faith has moved, the change your courage has created, and the glory your God has revealed. You are a walking, talking miracle. Even in the midst of your challenges, here you are, still believing, still working, still trusting.

I am so very proud of you.

160

I will not allow things I have no control over to have control over me. I am letting go and trusting God.

161

I believe with all my heart, spirit, and mind that my present will be greater than my past.

162

Today is not your day to give up.

And, to be clear, tomorrow isn't either.

163

Be courageously you.

All of you, not *some* of you.

164

She no longer did just enough to stay above water,
she decided it was time to walk on it.

She no longer did just enough to appear successful,
she decided it was time to be fulfilled.

165

This story ends with me in an Uber, heading home to Pooler, Georgia, (where I lived at the time) from my business trip in Atlanta.

The gentleman who picked me up looked to be in his sixties, and I distinctly remember jumping into the backseat with my suitcase and seeing that his car seats were covered in a loud hunting design.

"Do you like hunting?" I asked, to break the ice.

He chuckled and replied, "Ah yeah! Do you like tea?"

We laughed together as the conversation transitioned to each of us sharing a page or two of our stories, which led him to reveal he was a pastor. He took a trip down memory lane and told me about his old church, his love for helping people, and his life in Georgia.

"So what do you do?" he asked me.

I told him I was a marketing specialist by trade but that my passion has always been writing. He then asked me what I wrote about and what I loved most about writing. Digging deeper beneath the surface of my true feelings, I told him about my internal battle with becoming an author and the sign I had received from God in the form of Chris's message on LinkedIn.

Words kept flowing from my mouth as I shared my unexpected encounter with Chris. Before I knew it, we had made it to my destination, just as I was all out of words to speak.

He chuckled in amazement as he processed my experience. Then, he turned back to look me directly in the eyes and said,

"My prayer for you is grace."

"For the grace to be who you were created to be and do what you were created to do—*with joy*."

I thanked him and took his prayer with me as I rolled my luggage to my front door. I turned the key and opened the door to a welcoming home. Before taking another step, I smiled in awe as I whispered the words, "God is real."

***

God is faithful, and our lives are already accounted for, but we must invest in the process to experience His promises brought to life.

As you get ready to close this book, I must extend that same prayer to you—with my own little twist.

My prayer for you is one of courageous grace.

For the grace to be you with courage and do what you were created to do with courage.

Let joy radiate through your work, your rest, and the love you give others.

May you love yourself deeply and truly.

Show up each day in this world like you mean it, and go live out the assignment you were purposefully knitted together to fulfill.

I write these words with a deep sense of peace, because it is the end.

But how amazing is it to know it is the beginning of what I have always dreamed?

So, cheers, Dear Purposeful Woman, to courage and the lifelong pursuit of living freely and releasing all that we were created to.

You see, she found her way in the end.

And just like that, she trusted herself enough to finish what she started.

Smiling, she picked up her pen and repeated the process again.

To be continued . . .

About the author:

Shandice Stallworth is a daring thinker, deep feeler, and purpose-driven writer devoted to helping women courageously transform their lives from the inside out.

She cares about women's voices—she cares about women breaking through the walls of their past, pain, and insecurities to create a life that radiates their God-given purpose.

Shandice is a born and raised Londoner navigating life in Atlanta, Georgia, with her husband, Rodger, and a box full of journals.

Dear Purposeful Woman is her love letter to purposeful women all over the world who sometimes, like her, need a little nudge to walk in courage.

Keep the conversation going by sharing pictures of the words that speak to you the most: @dearpurposefulwoman #beyouwithcourage

Dear Purposeful Woman, I hope this book ignited something powerful within you. Spread the word, tear out pages you hold near and dear, and feel free to send me a message: hello@dearpurposefulwoman.com

We are family now. And I look forward to walking through Vol. 2 with you. – *Shandice Stallworth*

Made in the USA
Columbia, SC
25 April 2022